HEAD TO HEAD
GAMING HEROES

First published in Great Britain in 2025 by Welbeck Children's Books
An imprint of Hachette Children's Group

Copyright © 2025 Hodder & Stoughton Limited

All rights reserved. This book is sold subject to the condition that it
may not be reproduced, stored in a retrieval system, or transmitted
in any form or by any means, electronic, mechanical, photocopying,
recording, or otherwise, without the publisher's prior consent.

This book has not been authorised, licensed or endorsed by Nintendo Co., Ltd,
Sega Corporation, The Pokémon Company, Activision Blizzard, Inc., Insomniac
Games, Inc., Bandai Namco Entertainment Inc., Sony Interactive Entertainment
LLC, Mojang AB, Microsoft Corporation or any associated company.

ISBN 978 1 80453 882 1

Printed in China

10 9 8 7 6 5 4 3 2 1

Welbeck Children's Books
An imprint of Hachette Children's Group
Part of Hodder & Stoughton Limited
Carmelite House, 50 Victoria Embankment
London EC4Y 0DZ

An Hachette UK Company
www.hachette.co.uk
www.hachettechildrens.co.uk

The authorised representative in the EEA is Hachette Ireland, 8 Castlecourt
Centre, Dublin 15, D15 XTP3, Ireland (email: info@hbgi.ie)

HEAD TO HEAD
GAMING HEROES

WHO'S THE BEST GAMING CHARACTER?

YOU DECIDE!

WELBECK
CHILDREN'S BOOKS

CONTENTS

- **SPEEDY HEROES** 8
- **FIERCE FIGHTERS** 10
- **FIXER-UPPERS** 12
- **BEST ADVENTURE GAMES** 14
- **SUPER SIDEKICKS!** 16
- **BIG APPETITES!** 18
- **WISE RULERS** 20
- **BEST MARIO GAMES** 22
- **RAGING BULLIES** 24
- **GHOSTBUSTING** 26
- **ROBO-BUDDIES** 28
- **BEST RETRO GAMES** 30
- **FLY GUYS** 32
- **PUZZLE HEADS** 34

MOTOR RACERS	36
BEST RACING GAMES	38
CREATIVE MINDS	40
MULTI-TASKING	42
COOL DUDES	44
BEST GAME MOVIES	46
BIG BADS	48
ALL-ROUNDERS	50
TREASURE HUNTERS	52
BEST SONIC GAMES	54
PLANT LIFE	56
HIGH CLIMBERS	58
BEST POKÉMON PLAYTIME	60
CONSOLE CLASH!	62

TIME HER

Lots of different things can make someone a hero. It could be bravery, it could be cleverness.

Some heroes have superpowers, some have special skills — and some don't, but they try to do the right thing anyway!

FOR OES!

The world of gaming is full of heroes — so let's match some of them up against each other and ask who's best! The final decision...

IS YOURS!

SPEEDY HEROES
Blink and you'll miss them!

SONIC

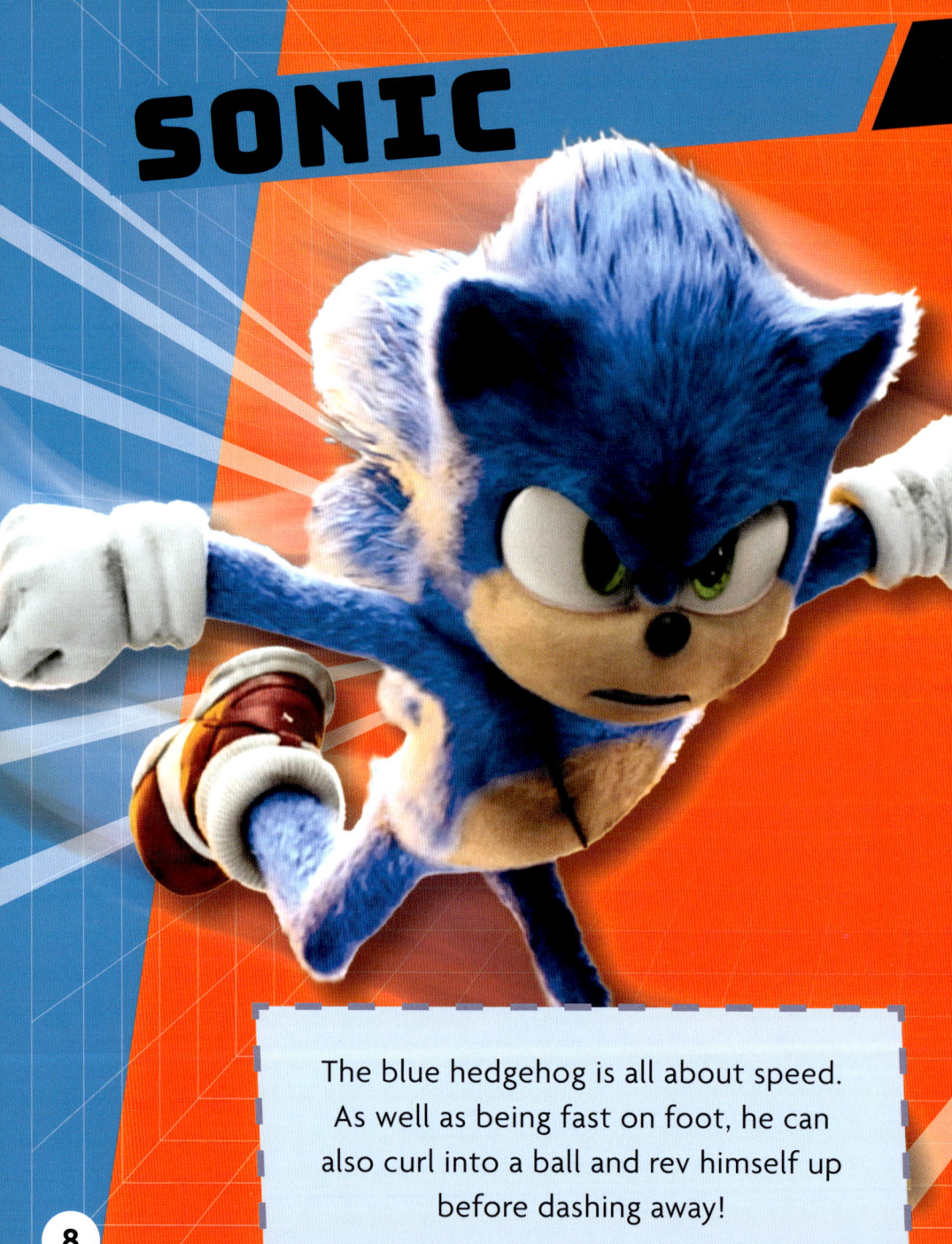

The blue hedgehog is all about speed. As well as being fast on foot, he can also curl into a ball and rev himself up before dashing away!

VS CRASH BANDICOOT

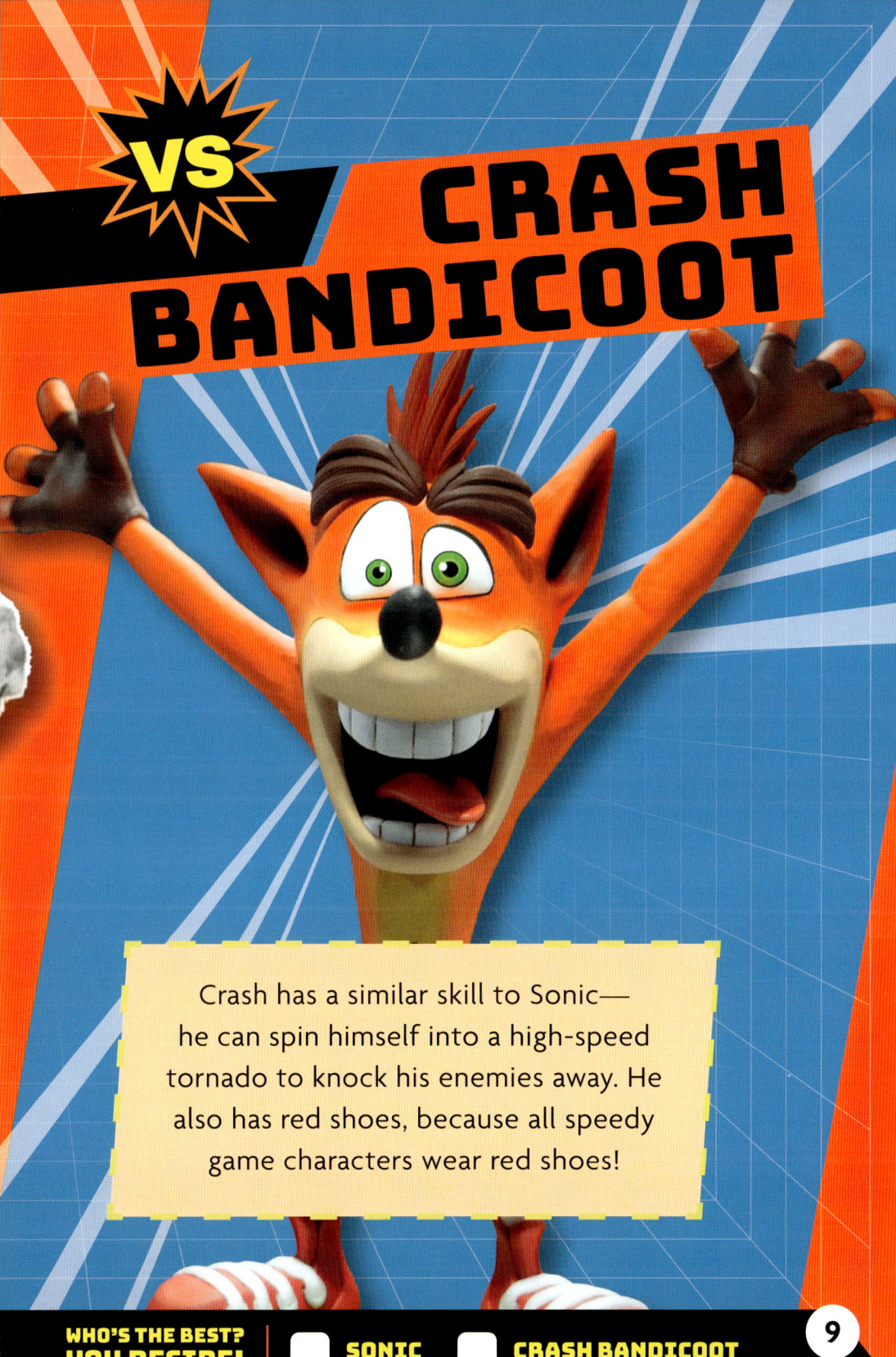

Crash has a similar skill to Sonic—he can spin himself into a high-speed tornado to knock his enemies away. He also has red shoes, because all speedy game characters wear red shoes!

WHO'S THE BEST? YOU DECIDE! ☐ SONIC ☐ CRASH BANDICOOT

FIERCE FIGHTERS
Who's got your back in a battle?

PIKACHU

Pikachu has a range of electrical attacks, and has been trained for combat. He can also evolve into the more powerful Raichu form!

VS LINK

Link is known as the finest swordsman in the kingdom of Hyrule, and has defeated many enemies who are much bigger than him. He's also handy with a crossbow!

WHO'S THE BEST? YOU DECIDE! ☐ PIKACHU ☐ LINK

FIXER-UPPERS
Both handy with a toolkit!

MARIO

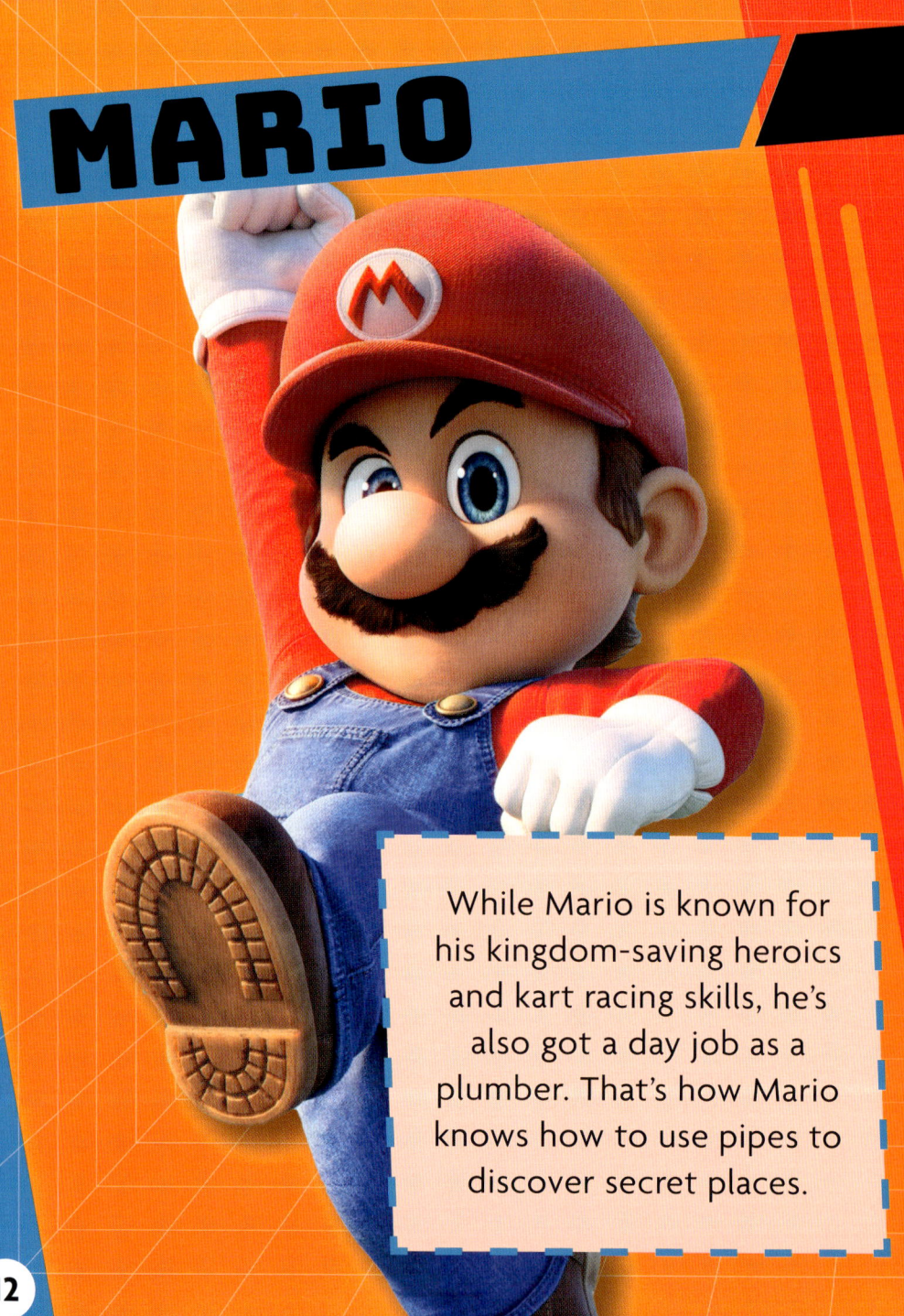

While Mario is known for his kingdom-saving heroics and kart racing skills, he's also got a day job as a plumber. That's how Mario knows how to use pipes to discover secret places.

VS RATCHET

Mechanic Ratchet can fix up spaceships. He loves gadgets, and his main tool is his oversized Omniwrench! He also meets a mysterious Plumber in several games...

WHO'S THE BEST? YOU DECIDE! ☐ MARIO ☐ RATCHET

BEST ADVENTURE GAMES

Because heroes are at their best when they've got a quest!

5
RATCHET & CLANK: RIFT APART

The pals team up once again to take on an interdimensional emperor looking to conquer the universe!

4
PIKMIN 4

These are some of the most creative games around, and this one has a cute kinda dog thing!

3
KIRBY AND THE FORGOTTEN LAND

The cute pink guy goes on a surprisingly spooky quest in an abandoned world!

2
ASTRO BOT

The cute robo-dude goes on an epic adventure to rescue his friends! Everyone with a PS5 should own this game.

1
THE LEGEND OF ZELDA: ECHOES OF WISDOM

Usually Link is the main character in The Legend of Zelda, but Princess Zelda finally gets to star in this game where magic is more important than combat!

SUPER SIDEKICKS!
Who's the best sidekick?

LUIGI

Luigi is Mario's loyal brother. He's always got Mario's back, and even knows how to have his own adventures too, in Luigi's Mansion!

VS TAILS

Tails is Sonic's best friend. He's a genius inventor and can use his two tails to fly, helping to get Sonic and his other friends to safety!

WHO'S THE BEST? YOU DECIDE! ☐ LUIGI ☐ TAILS

BIG APPETITES!
Who's the hungriest?

YOSHI

Yoshi loves eating fruit, items and enemies, especially when he's carrying Baby Mario on his back! Sometimes he spits them back out, but he can swallow them and use them to make eggs!

VS KIRBY

Kirby can vacuum up all kinds of enemies and power-ups, despite his small size! If he swallows enemies or special items, he takes on their abilities!

WHO'S THE BEST? YOU DECIDE! ☐ YOSHI ☐ KIRBY

WISE RULERS
Which princess runs her kingdom the best?

PEACH

The ruler of the Mushroom Kingdom, Peach used to get kidnapped a lot, but these days she's more often seen exploring and fighting alongside Mario— or having her own adventures!

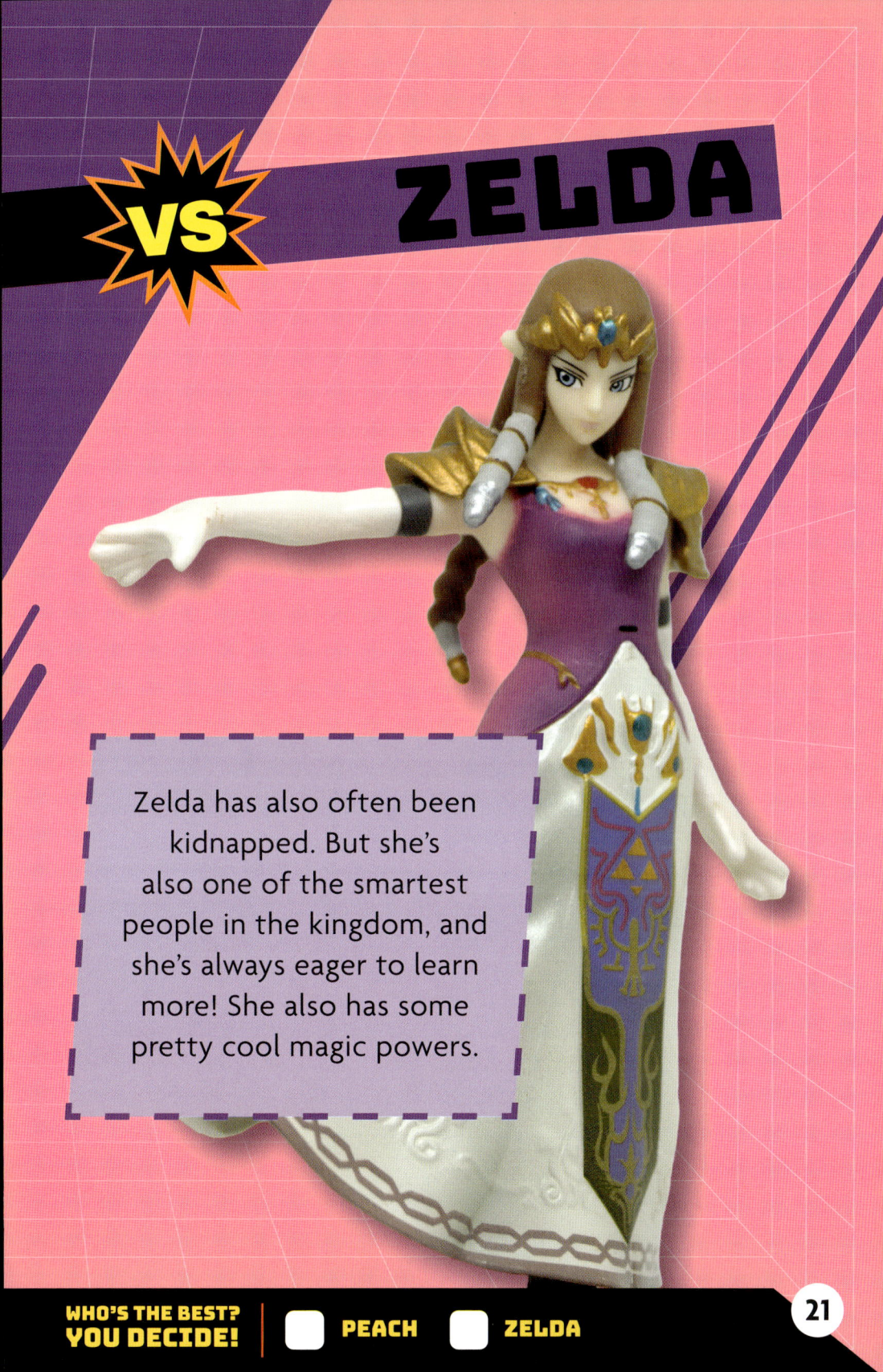

VS ZELDA

Zelda has also often been kidnapped. But she's also one of the smartest people in the kingdom, and she's always eager to learn more! She also has some pretty cool magic powers.

WHO'S THE BEST? YOU DECIDE! ☐ PEACH ☐ ZELDA

BEST MARIO GAMES

The plum games starring the plumber and his pals!

5
SUPER MARIO BROS. 3

This was a big leap forward for the Mario games, with lots of levels to explore and the awesome Tanooki Suit!

4
SUPER MARIO GALAXY

You can find this cosmic epic on the Super Mario 3D All-Stars collection!

3
DONKEY KONG COUNTRY

The game that took Donkey Kong from hero to villain! He's joined by Diddy Kong as they try to take back their banana stash.

2
SUPER MARIO ODYSSEY

A huge adventure, where you can use Mario's hat to control objects and other characters!

1
SUPER MARIO BROS. WONDER

This is one of the most creative Mario games ever made, with lots of secrets to find. You can also transform into an elephant!

RAGING BULLIES
Which of Mario's enemies is angriest?

DONKEY KONG

The great ape has starred in many of his own games, using his strength to defeat the crocodile invaders of his island. Having your bananas stolen would drive anyone bananas!

VS WARIO

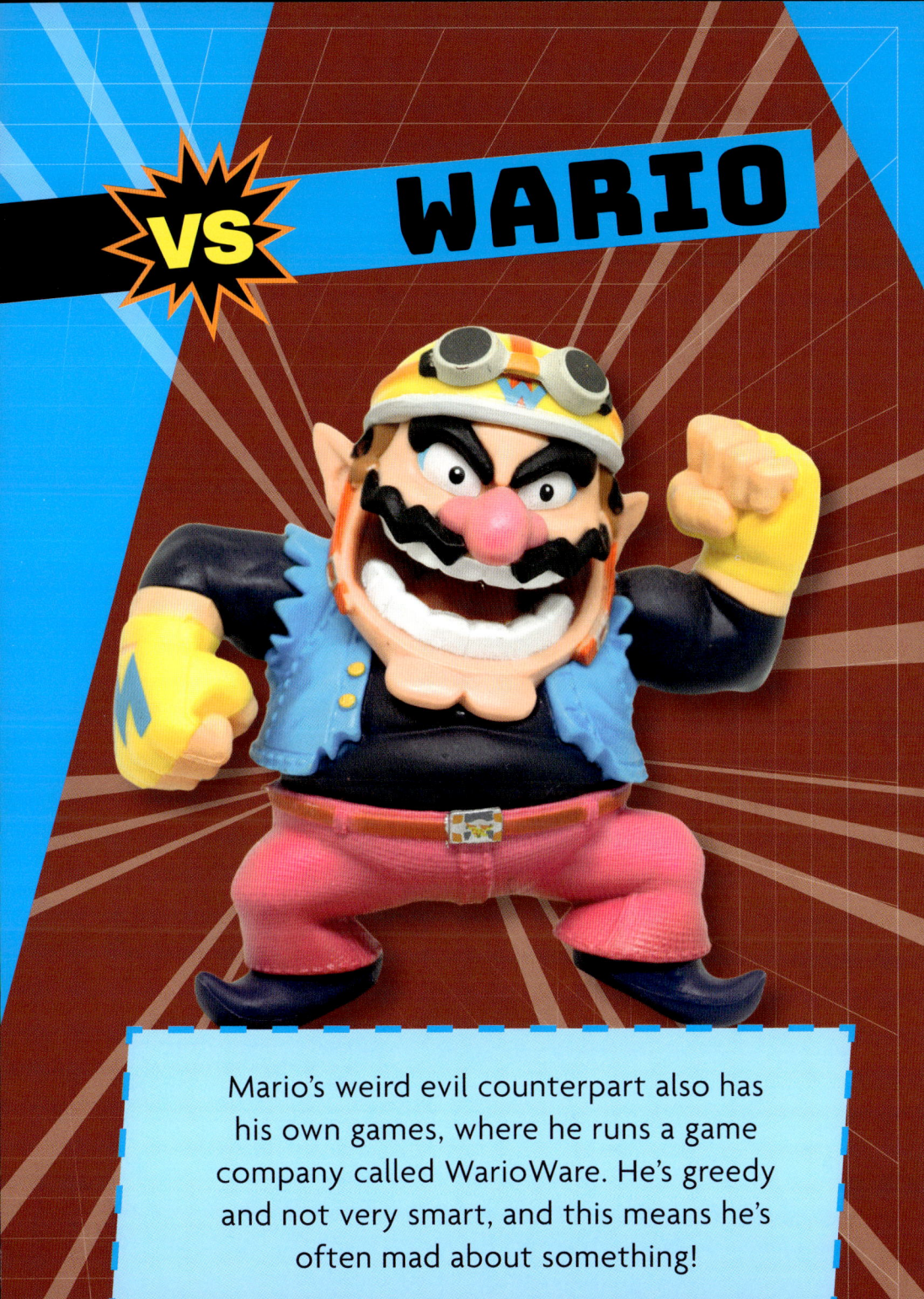

Mario's weird evil counterpart also has his own games, where he runs a game company called WarioWare. He's greedy and not very smart, and this means he's often mad about something!

WHO'S THE BEST? YOU DECIDE! ☐ DONKEY KONG ☐ WARIO

GHOSTBUSTING
Who doesn't get spooked easily?

LUIGI

In the Luigi's Mansion games, Luigi faces his fears by tackling big old houses full of ghosts, using a special vacuum cleaner, the Poltergust 3000!

VS PAC-MAN

Most of the time, Pac-Man avoids the ghosts that chase him around mazes—but if he gets a power-up, the tables are turned and he can chase them!

WHO'S THE BEST? YOU DECIDE! ☐ LUIGI ☐ PAC-MAN

ROBO-BUDDIES
Who's the best 'bot in a crisis?

CLANK

Clank is an intelligent but faulty robot who escapes from a war-bot factory and teams up with Ratchet to stop an evil businessman. He's more heroic than Ratchet, to be honest!

VS ASTRO BOT

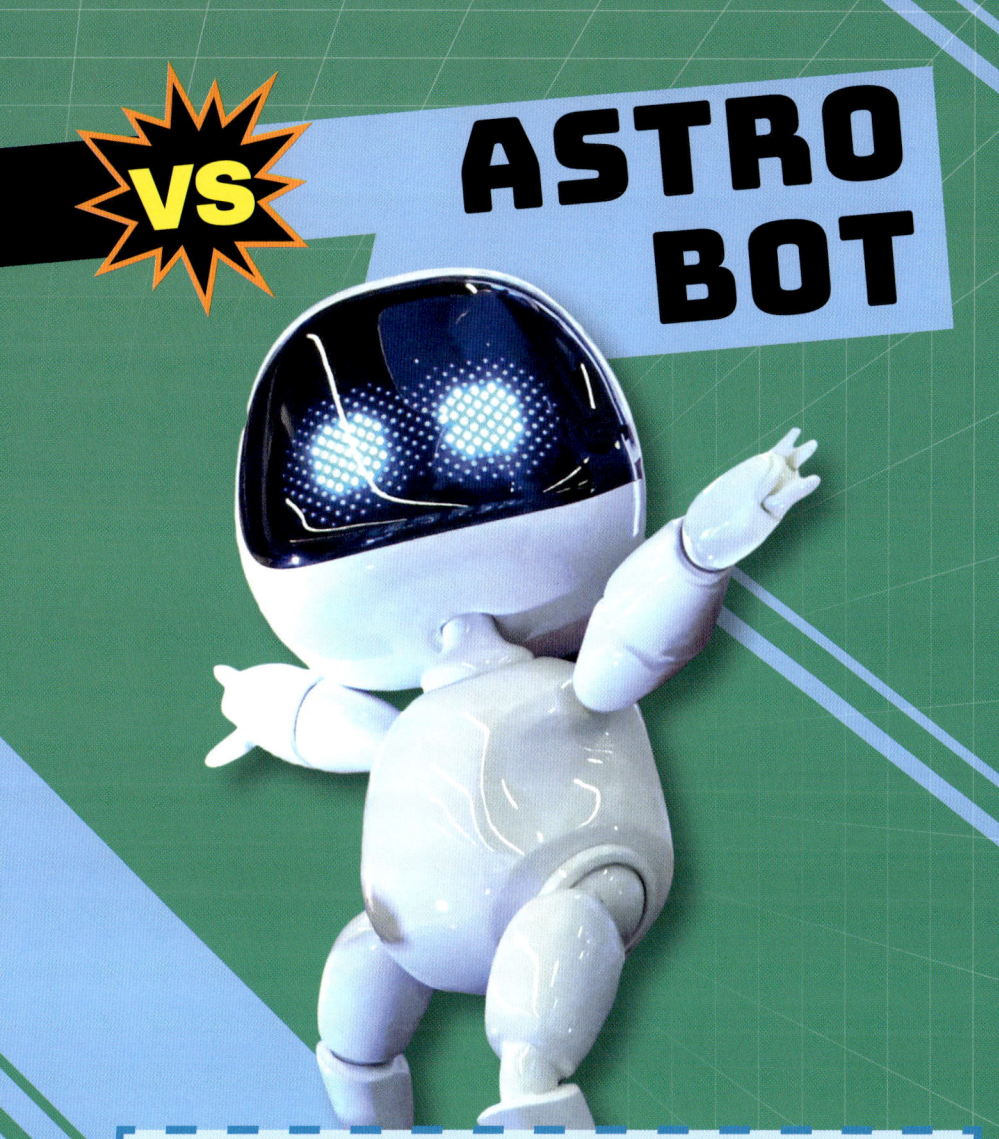

This little guy is a space explorer who rescues his friends when they get scattered across different planets by the alien, Space Bully Nebulax! He can learn lots of different skills.

WHO'S THE BEST? YOU DECIDE! ☐ CLANK ☐ ASTRO BOT

BEST RETRO GAMES

Let's go old-school!

5 PILOTWINGS

Keep your cool to pass the tests at this flight school!

4 PAC-MAN

Still so addictive, but like a lot of older games, it's tricky!

3 HARVEST MOON

This really chill farming game has been copied by a lot of others since it came out!

2 THE LEGEND OF ZELDA: LINK'S AWAKENING

This was made for the original Game Boy, and it's one of Link's most magical adventures, as he washes up on a strange island!

1 KIRBY'S ADVENTURE

This was made for the NES, and it's got so many awesome ideas in it. It'll make you smile!

FLY GUYS
The winner of this battle is up in the air!

KIRBY

The pink fella flies by taking a big gulp of air to blow himself up like a balloon, and then flapping his arms like crazy. He can hold his breath a long time!

VS TAILS

Sonic's sidekick can spin his twin tails to make him go faster—but he can also spin them like helicopter blades. How come they don't get tangled up? We don't know!

WHO'S THE BEST? YOU DECIDE! ☐ KIRBY ☐ TAILS

PUZZLE HEADS
They'll find the answers!

CAPTAIN OLIMAR

This spacefarer crash-landed on a strange planet, where he discovered Pikmin, tiny plant-creatures. By giving jobs to the Pikmin, he managed to solve tricky problems and repair his ship!

VS DETECTIVE PIKACHU

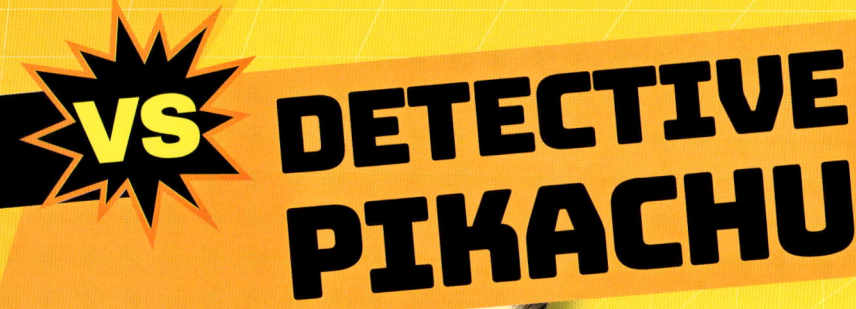

When there's a mystery in the world of Pokémon, a Pikachu in a deerstalker hat is the guy you need to solve it! He works with his human sidekick, Tim Goodman.

WHO'S THE BEST? YOU DECIDE! ☐ OLIMAR ☐ PIKACHU

MOTOR RACERS
Start your engines for the ultimate kart-off!

MARIO

When he's not plumbing or adventuring, Mario's a keen sportsman, playing tennis, golf, soccer, baseball, and more—but he's the absolute king of kart racing!

VS CRASH BANDICOOT

Crash doesn't just race for fun—he and his friends are also trying to save the Earth from N. Oxide, who wants to concrete over the world and turn it into a parking lot!

WHO'S THE BEST? YOU DECIDE! MARIO CRASH BANDICOOT

BEST RACING GAMES

Start your engines!

5 DISNEY SPEEDSTORM

This free-to-play racer lets you choose from a whole range of Disney and Pixar characters!

4 WIPEOUT

This futuristic racer is super fast and super cool! There's a great remaster called Wipeout Omega Collection on the PlayStation.

3 TEAM SONIC RACING

In this game you can work as a team, sending powerups to your partner!

2 CRASH TEAM RACING

The original Crash Team Racing has also had a remaster for modern consoles. It's great fun, but gets tricky very quickly!

1 MARIO KART 8 DELUXE

Featuring souped-up versions of classic tracks from across the series, this is the ultimate Mario Kart experience.

CREATIVE MINDS
Thinking outside the box!

SACKBOY

In LittleBigPlanet you play as Sackboy and can create levels of your own, using the stuff you've collected while playing the story mode. With Sackboy, you can make any type of game you like!

VS STEVE

The default character in Minecraft can build almost anything, if he can get the right materials—but it might be a bit square-looking! You'd definitely want him around if you were stranded in the middle of nowhere.

WHO'S THE BEST? YOU DECIDE! ☐ SACKBOY ☐ STEVE

MULTI-TASKING
Who's good at learning new tricks?

PEACH

In Princess Peach: Showtime!, the ruler of the Mushroom Kingdom travels into different worlds where she becomes a swordfighter, a ninja, a cowgirl, a figure skater, a detective and more!

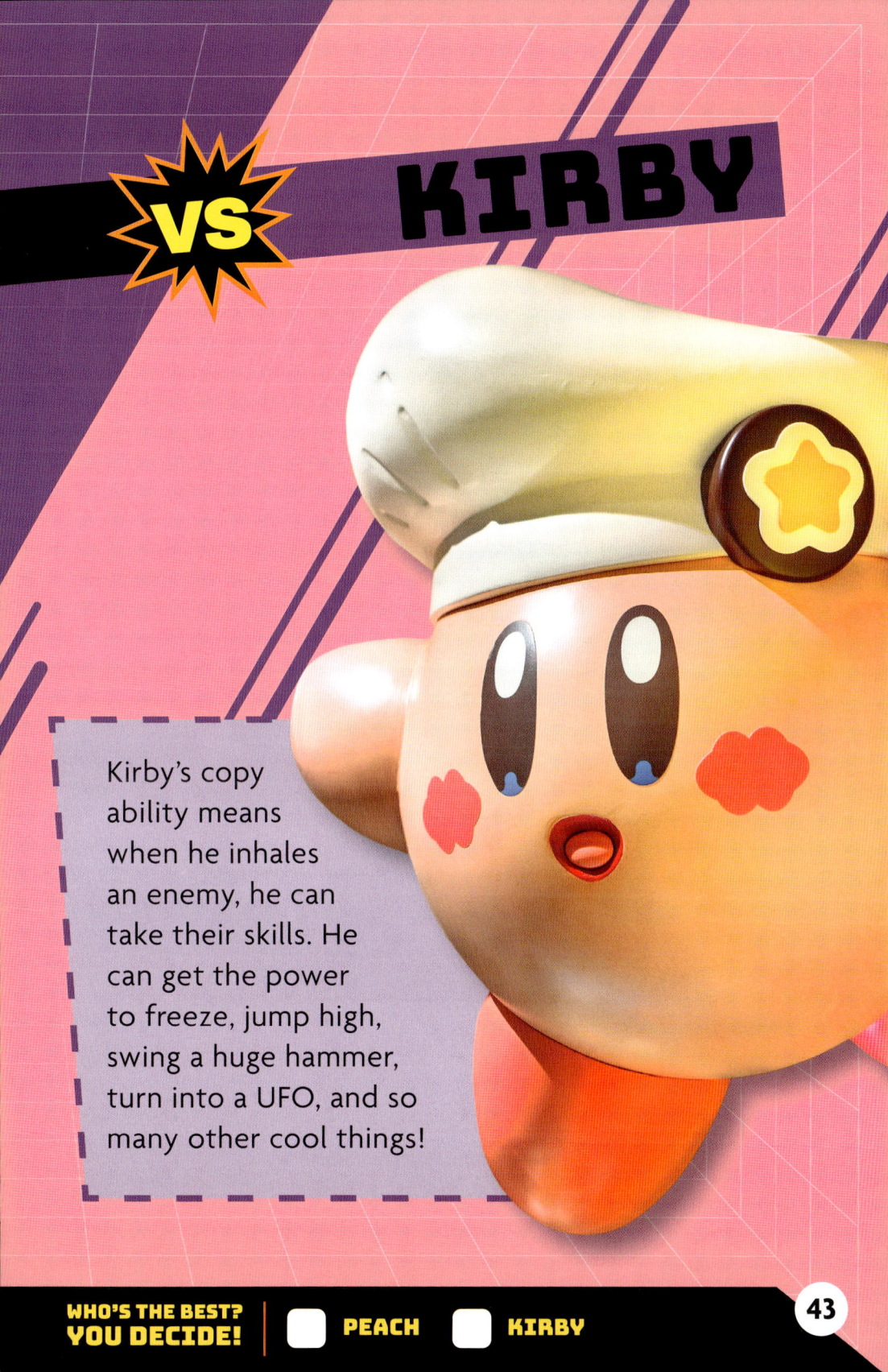

VS KIRBY

Kirby's copy ability means when he inhales an enemy, he can take their skills. He can get the power to freeze, jump high, swing a huge hammer, turn into a UFO, and so many other cool things!

WHO'S THE BEST? YOU DECIDE! ☐ PEACH ☐ KIRBY

COOL DUDES
Two pretty slick guys, here!

SHADOW

Motorbike-riding Shadow the Hedgehog was only meant to appear in Sonic Adventure 2, but was so popular he became a regular part of the games and also got a game of his own!

VS RATCHET

He can be selfish and over-confident at times, but Ratchet's heart is in the right place, he has some nifty skills, and he's very cool in a crisis!

WHO'S THE BEST? YOU DECIDE! ☐ SHADOW ☐ RATCHET

BEST GAME MOVIES

Stars of the silver screen!

5
THE ANGRY BIRDS MOVIE

Who knew there was a whole movie in this simple mobile game?

4
RATCHET & CLANK

A movie based on their epic space adventures was a perfect idea!

3
SONIC THE HEDGEHOG

Almost thirty years after the first game, this movie made Sonic big news all over again!

2
DETECTIVE PIKACHU

The first live-action film to be set in the Pokémon world is this mystery with a dark side!

1
THE SUPER MARIO BROS. MOVIE

This film brought together everything that makes the Mario games great. We love Bowser's song!

BIG BADS
These guys have all the evil plans!

DR ROBOTNIK

Also known as Dr Eggman, and played by Jim Carrey in the movies, this mad scientist imprisoned animals inside robot casings and made them into his minions! In Sonic 2 he also has a huge sky fortress…

VS BOWSER

Mario's arch-enemy is a big angry turtle, the king of the Koopas. He also has a sky fortress—a flying castle. His plans are often based around kidnapping Princess Peach.

WHO'S THE BEST? YOU DECIDE! ☐ DR ROBOTNIK ☐ BOWSER

ALL-ROUNDERS
Who's the roundest of these heroes?

PAC-MAN

One of the first gaming heroes, Pac-Man was designed to be a simple shape: a yellow circle with a mouth! He's still one of the most recognizable characters in games.

KIRBY

Nintendo wanted a new, super-cute character, so they made him a ball with arms and feet. His first game was on the green screen Game Boy, so he didn't become pink until his second game!

WHO'S THE BEST? YOU DECIDE! ☐ PAC-MAN ☐ KIRBY

TREASURE HUNTERS
These guys can't resist shiny things!

SONIC

Sonic collects gold rings scattered across the Zones of his world, which protect him from harm—but he must also find the powerful Chaos Emeralds that can turn him into Super Sonic!

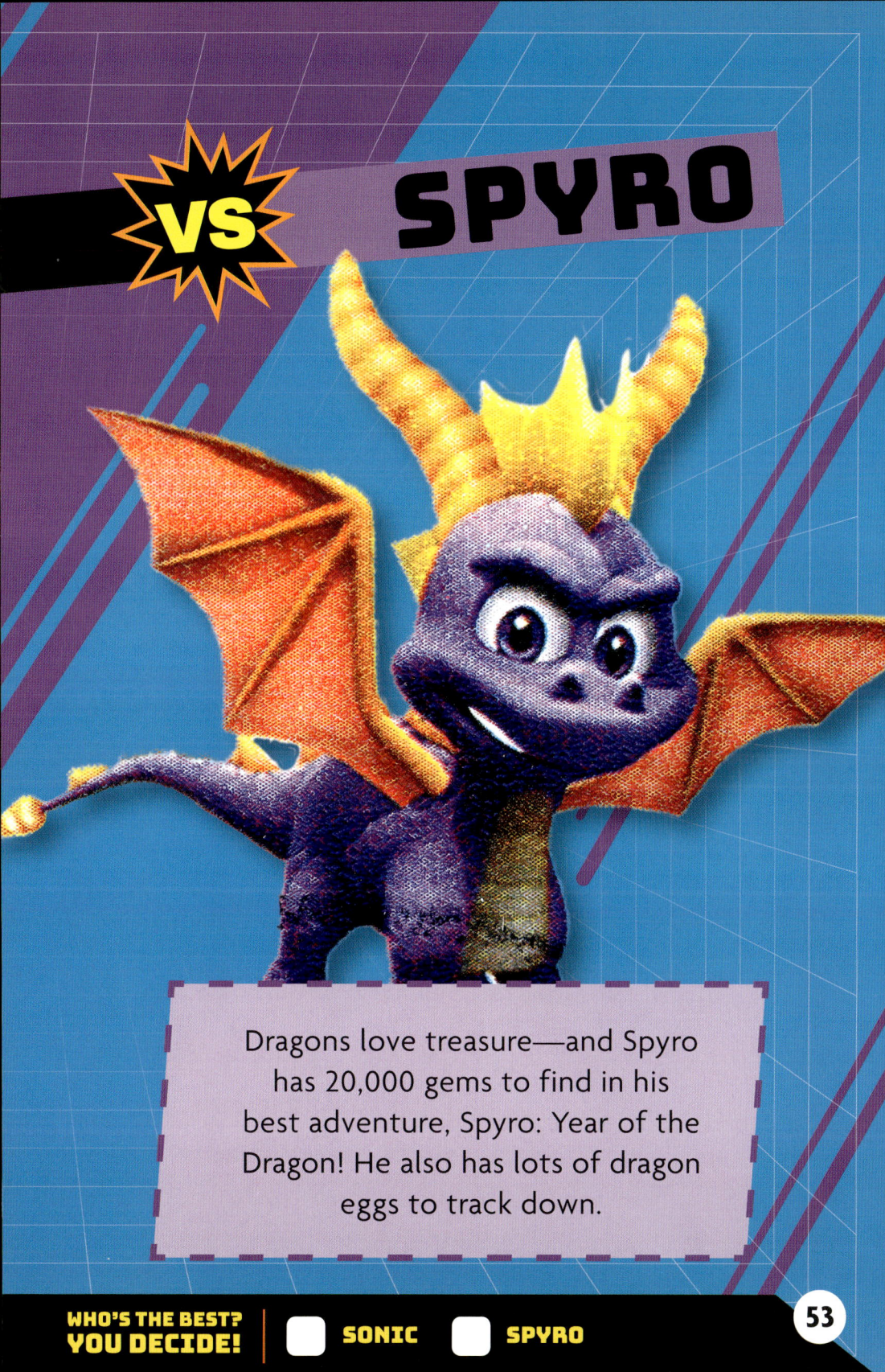

BEST SONIC GAMES

The fastest games in town!

5 SONIC ADVENTURE 2
Sonic usually works better in 2D than 3D, but this game is great!

4 SONIC MANIA
This mixes up new versions of classic zones with some amazing new stages!

3
SONIC THE HEDGEHOG 2

All the early Sonic games are awesome, but this has the coolest music and some really tricky special stages!

2
SONIC SUPERSTARS

Classic Sonic and modern Sonic come together to make an awesome celebration of the series!

1
SONIC 3 & KNUCKLES

This is so big they made it into two separate games. But played together, they're unbeatable!

PLANT LIFE
Which of these garden-grown guys is tops?

TOAD

There are many mushroom people in the Mushroom Kingdom, but one of them, just called Toad (like a toadstool!), is more of a friend to Mario than most. He has even starred in his own games!

HIGH CLIMBERS
Walls are no obstacle for these guys!

KNUCKLES

The funky red echidna is slower than Sonic, but his spiked gloves give him an awesome grip that lets him climb up walls! Sonic should get some of those gloves.

VS LINK

In the earlier games, Link needed ladders to get off the ground—but in Breath of the Wild he can climb almost any surface, as long as he's got enough stamina to reach the top!

WHO'S THE BEST? YOU DECIDE! ☐ KNUCKLES ☐ LINK

BEST POKÉMON PLAYTIME

So many different ways to catch them all!

5 TOYS

Pokémon make the best plushies!

4 POKÉMON GO

The free-to-play mobile game lets you catch Pokémon in the real world. Watch where you're going, though!

3
MOVIES & TV

After 26 seasons of Ash battling his way to the top, a new series, Pokémon Horizons, started with new characters.

2
TRADING CARDS

The cards are cool and collectible—don't forget you can actually play a game with them too!

1
SWITCH GAMES

Detective Pikachu Returns, Let's Go, Pikachu! and Pokemon Snap are some of the best games you can buy on Switch.

CONSOLE CLASH!

Which platform comes out on top?

NINTENDO SWITCH

It's the only console you can play Mario, Kirby, Pokémon and Zelda games on – and you can take it with you wherever you go!

SONY PS5

The super-powerful PlayStation 5 has amazing graphics, and the Astro Bot games are some of the best around right now!

XBOX SERIES X/S

If you don't need your games on discs, the XBox comes in a special slim version. It's more aimed at older gamers though!

WHERE ARE THEY FROM?

Sonic the Hedgehog, Tails, Shadow, Dr. Robotnik, and **Knuckles** are from Sega's **Sonic the Hedgehog** game series.

Mario, Luigi, Yoshi, Princess Peach, Bowser, Toad, and **Wario** can be found in Nintendo's **Super Mario** games.

Link and **Zelda** are in Nintendo's **The Legend of Zelda** series.

Kirby is in the **Kirby** game series from Nintendo.

Captain Olimar and the **Pikmin** are from Nintendo's **Pikmin** series.

Donkey Kong is from Nintendo's **Donkey Kong** series (and he started out in a **Mario** game!)

Crash Bandicoot has his own series from Activision Blizzard, and **Spyro** is in Activision Blizzard's **Skylanders** games.

Pikachu and **Detective Pikachu** can be found in the **Pokémon** games.

Ratchet and Clank star in their own games from Insomniac Games, Inc.

You'll find **Pac-Man** in a variety of games from Bandai Namco Entertainment Inc.

Astro Bot has his own series of Sony games, and **Sackboy** is from the **LittleBigAdventure** series (he even got his own **Sackboy: A Big Adventure** game!)

Want to see more of **Steve**? You'll find him in **Minecraft**, from Mojang and Microsoft.

The publishers would like to thank the following sources for their kind permission to reproduce the pictures in this book.

ALAMY STOCK PHOTO: Abaca Press 29; Piotr Adamowicz 62; ArcadeImages 23T, 31T, 31B, 37, 38, 39T, 54, 55T; Album 35; Atlaspix 46; BFA 8, 12, 17, 33, 44, 47B; Chris Bardgett 39B, 57; Fernando Barrios 24; Collection Christophel 28; Michele D'Ottavio 30; DarkBarrios 10, 11, 21, 25, 34; DecaStock 63B; Entertainment Pictures 45; Everett Collection Inc 13, 42, 47T, 48; FlixPix 58; John Hanson Pye 50; M4OS Photos 41; Patti McConville 49; Stepan Popov 23B; Hugh Threlfall 63T; Chris Willson 52; Cliff Wong 19, 20, 26, 27, 36; Boris Zhitkov 16, 18, 56

GETTY IMAGES: Juniorbeep 40; Stanislav Kogiku/SOPA Images/LightRocket 59

SHUTTERSTOCK: BH-Photo 22; Eric Broder Van Dyke 15T; Riccio da favola 61B; FeLopes 14; Frantisek Jarabica 9; KateV28 15B; KeongDaGreat 60B; Kraft74 60T; Kuremo 43, 51; RINDAWS 61T; Priyanshu Sarate 32; Spatuletail 53; Travers Lewis 55B